DISCOVER SCIENCE

WATER

Kim Taylor

Chrysalis Children's Books

DISCOVER ● SCIENCE

Contents

First published in the UK in 2003 by
Chrysalis Children's Books
An imprint of Chrysalis Books Group Plc, The Chrysalis Building, Bramley Road London W10 6SP

Paperback edition first published in 2005

ISBN 1 84138 622 7 (hb)
ISBN 1 84458 451 8 (pb)

Designed by Robin Wright, Times Four Publishing Ltd

Illustrated by Guy Smith

Science adviser: Richard Oels, Warden Park School, Cuckfield, Sussex

Typeset by Amber Graphics, Burgess Hill
Printed in China

About this book

This book will tell you many intriguing things about water. It will tell you what water is made of, where it comes from and where it goes to. You can find out how clouds are made, why it rains, and what happens when water freezes or boils. On every page there are fascinating photographs to show you what water is like as it flows, freezes, spins, splashes and bubbles.

Each topic is accompanied by a simple experiment that will help you have fun while finding out more about water.

Do you know how much water a large tree drinks in one day? Do you know why you can't make a cup of tea at the top of a high mountain? In this book you will find the answers to these and other interesting questions.

The world of water

Planet Earth is a watery place. More than 70 per cent of its surface is covered by water, most of it in deep, salty oceans. There is also a great deal of fresh, non-salty, water. This is found in the air, soaked into the ground, frozen into ice or flowing in rivers, lakes and streams. Because there is so much water around, it is easy to forget how very important it is. Without it, the Earth would be a desert. Every single plant and animal – including every human being – would die without water.

Water go-round

Water is on the move all the time. The sun warms the sea, which makes tiny particles of water rise up into the air. This is called **evaporation**. The mixture of water particles and air is called water **vapour.**

As it rises the water vapour cools, so that the vapour turns back into water drops. These drops eventually fall to earth as rain, which trickles down mountains, into streams and rivers, and so returns again to the sea.

What is water?

Everyone knows what water is – it's a clear, colourless liquid, isn't it? But that's only part of the story. Water is not always liquid. If you cool it, it becomes ice – which is solid. If you heat it, it becomes steam – which is a gas. In fact, water is made from a mixture of two different kinds of gas, **hydrogen** and **oxygen**. If these gases are mixed together and lit with a match, there is a flash of blue flame and a loud pop and all that is left are a few drops of water.

Did you know?

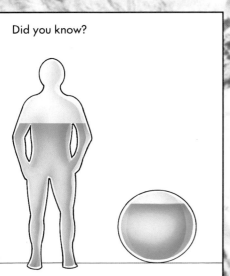

Your body is about 61 per cent water. A melon is more than 95 per cent water!

Water experiment

THE AMAZING NODDING WATER BIRD

1 Cut the bird shape as shown from the piece of plastic. Make a hole through the middle of its body.

2 Cut a strip of blotting paper with a tuft for the bird's head and Sellotape it to the neck of bird. Leave 10mm below the body.

3 Push the needle through the hole. Fix it each side with Plasticine.

4 Weight the body with Plasticine so that the bird will just balance upright on the glass.

5 Pour water into the glass until the end of the blotting paper touches the surface.

You need
- A plastic carton lid
- A darning needle
- A glass
- Plasticine
- Sellotape

Plasticine

The blotting paper soaks up water which rises to the bird's head, making it top heavy so that it nods forward. Evaporation dries the blotting paper until the bird sits up, wetting its tail again.

Wet air

The air you breathe is not completely dry. You cannot see the water vapour in it, but some is always there. Warm air can hold more water than cold air. So, if warm air full of water cools down, the extra water in it has to escape somehow. It does this by turning to liquid and forming tiny droplets. This is called **condensing**.

Water has to condense *on* to something. In the morning you can often see droplets, called dew, on grass. This happens when air cools near the ground at night and water droplets condense onto the grass. You can also see water droplets on windows in warm houses. The droplets form when hot air in a heated room meets the cold glass of the window.

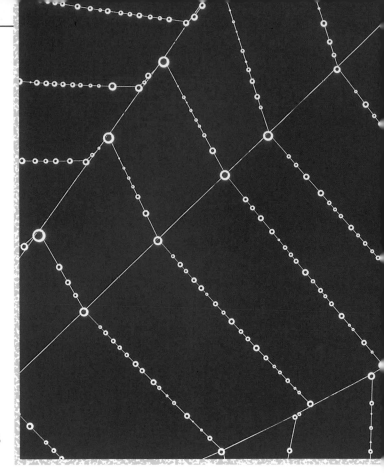

As water from the air condenses, dew forms on this spider's web.

How air gets wet

If you leave a damp sponge overnight, it may be dry by morning. This is because the water in the sponge has evaporated. In the same way, water in the ground, in lakes, rivers and oceans is evaporating all the time. The sun helps water to evaporate by warming the air so that it can hold a lot of water. But water can also evaporate into cold dry air. Even ice and snow evaporate. A lot of snow that falls on high mountains never melts – it just evaporates.

Warm air, which is full of water, condenses in droplets when it touches a glass of cold drink.

6

Water experiment

WET OR DRY?

You need
● A pine cone

1 Place the pine cone outside, sheltered from the sun and rain. When the air is wet, the cone will be closed.

2 If you bring the cone into a warm room where the air is dry, it will open up.

It will take several hours or even days for the cone to open or close fully.

Cloud, mist and fog

Cloud, mist and fog are all made of the same thing: millions of tiny droplets of water floating in the air. The droplets form when wet air cools. As it cools, the air cannot hold all its vapour any more and so some condenses into a cloud of droplets.

Fog and mist form near the ground when warm wet air meets and mixes with colder air. Clouds develop high above the ground when warm wet air, which rises during the day or is blown up the sides of mountains, meets colder air higher up.

Rain

Clouds are made of millions of very tiny droplets of water or equally tiny ice crystals. The droplets are like dust, so small that they do not fall but just drift about. If the cloud is cooled, more water from the air condenses onto the droplets and they begin to grow in size.

As the droplets get bigger and heavier they start to fall – slowly at first. They gather more water from the air and go on growing. Now the droplets begin to feel like **drizzle**, which is very fine rain. If the cloud is very high above the ground, the drops have a long way to fall. As they fall they get bigger and bigger and fall faster and faster until they come pelting down onto the ground as really heavy rain.

Natural raincoats

Many creatures have natural raincoats. Rain runs off birds' feathers because they are **waterproof**. Some animals have waterproof fur.

Rain clouds often have rounded tops like cotton wool. They may form at the tops of mountains or hills which lift up the air and cool it.

When clouds rise they get cooler. As they cool, the water vapour they contain begins to condense into drops which fall as rain.

Ducks swim in a pond as the rain falls around them. Their skin is dry and warm beneath their waterproof feathers.

Water experiment

MEASURE YOUR RAINFALL!

1 Put the glass jar outside in the open.

2 Place the plastic funnel in the top of the jar.

The rain collects in the glass jar. You can use a ruler to measure how much rain has fallen in a night or over several days or even weeks. By using a rain gauge like this one, you can keep a record of the rainfall throughout the year.

You need
- A plastic funnel
- A straight sided glass jar about the same diameter as the top of the funnel

Rainstorms

The biggest rainstorms happen in hot countries. Because the air is so warm, it can hold a lot of water vapour. When this warm wet air rises and cools, terrific rainstorms develop. The clouds are so high that the drops have a long way to fall. When they reach the ground they are really big and come smacking down.

Seen from a distance, rain looks like a grey sheet hanging from a cloud.

Freezing

When water is cooled below 0°C, it changes from a liquid to a solid called ice. Like lots of other solids, ice is made up of crystals. You can see ice crystals forming on a puddle when the weather turns frosty. They are shaped like knife blades and can be several centimetres long. As the puddle freezes over, the crystals join together into a solid layer of ice. Icicles form from dripping water. As water trickles down the outside of an icicle to the tip, it freezes into a thin layer of ice making the icicle fatter and longer.

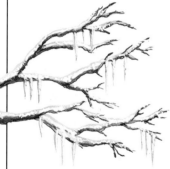

Ice

Ice is frozen water. It takes a lot of cooling to change water into ice even when the water is already at 0°C. Similarly, it takes a lot of heat to melt ice and change it from ice at 0°C to water at 0°C. Heat is not the only thing that melts ice. Pressure also melts it. That is how a **glacier** – a river of ice – can flow down a mountain. Where the pressure of the rocks squeezes the ice, it melts a little and begins to move.

A glacier flows down a mountain and then breaks into icebergs when it reaches the sea.

Life under ice

Freezing makes water expand, which means it gets bigger. That is why ice always floats on the surface of a pond. If ice sank, a pond would quickly freeze into a solid block, starting at the bottom. So it is lucky for fish that ice floats. They can swim about safely in the cold water beneath the ice where there is plenty of oxygen for them to breathe. When the weather turns warmer, the ice slowly melts from solid to liquid and the fish can come up to the surface to feed again.

These goldfish are able to survive under the ice where the water is warmer.

Did you know?

Over 90% of the fresh water on the Earth's surface consists of glaciers.

Water experiment

MAKE ICE COLDER

1 Put six ice cubes into the bowl and measure the temperature which should be about 0°C.

2 Scatter a teaspoon of salt on to the ice cubes.

3 Measure the temperature again and you will find that it is lower! The melting ice uses up heat but the salt provides none. Therefore the ice has to take more heat from itself, which lowers the temperature further.

You need
- A glass bowl
- Ice cubes
- Cooking salt
- A thermometer reading to -20°C

Snow

Snowflakes are made of tiny ice cystals that form from water vapour high up in the clouds. The crystals floating in the air are attracted to each other and join up to form flakes which then begin to fall, getting bigger as they come down. Snow is different from frozen rain. When rain freezes it falls in large icy drops called hail. Fresh snow, on the other hand, is light and fluffy. Snow that is 10cm deep contains about the same amount of water as 1 cm of rain.

There are ice crystals sparkling in this fresh snow.

Boiling

When water is heated to a temperature of 100°C it boils. This means it turns into a gas called steam. You cannot see steam because it is clear. What you see above a boiling saucepan is steam condensing into a cloud of tiny droplets. As the cloud drifts away the droplets evaporate until all that is left is water vapour in the air, which you can't see.

Just as ice takes a lot of heat to melt, so water needs a lot of heat to turn it to steam, even when it has reached its boiling point.

A jet of boiling water bursts out of a geyser in Africa.

Steam from the spout of a coffee pot condenses to form a cloud.

Hot springs

Deep in the ground the rocks are very hot. If water seeps into hot rocks it tries to boil, but the great pressure underground may stop it. In some places boiling water and steam burst out of the ground as a **geyser**.

Boiling point

Water normally boils at 100°C, which is called its boiling point. At this temperature it will cook an egg and make a cup of tea. But the boiling point is not fixed. Water under pressure can get much hotter before it starts to boil. That is how pressure cookers work. Inside, water reaches 120°C before it starts to boil and the food cooks faster. Pressure squeezes the water so that steam bubbles cannot form. Even outside a pressure cooker, pressure from the atmosphere is trying to stop bubbles forming. In space or in a vacuum, where there is no pressure, water will boil from the heat of your hand.

Water experiment

SPOT THE WATER DROPLETS!

Warning!
You must be very careful when doing this experiment because steam can be hot! Ask an adult to help you.

Shine the torch towards you from behind the steam. As the steam drifts up you should be able to see the tiny water droplets.

Steam power

When water is heated so that it turns to steam, it expands enormously. The steam can be used in an engine to drive it along. As the steam expands it pushes pistons in and out, and these make the wheels go round.

Mixing

Some solids, such as sugar or salt, mix with water completely. This is called **dissolving**, and the mixture is called a **solution**. However long you leave a sugar solution, the sugar will not separate from the water – unless, of course, the water evaporates. Clay and mud do not dissolve. If you mix them with water and then leave the mixture to stand, the clay and mud fall to the bottom in a layer of **sediment**.

Mud mixed with water in the Tana River, Kenya.

Liquid layers

Oil and water do not mix. Oil floats in a layer on top of water. If you shake them together, both may break up into round drops called **globules**. The oil globules float to the surface of the water where they join up with each other again. You can see water globules in the oil layer in the picture.

If you shake oil and water together very hard, the globules become tiny and do not join together. Oil and water mixed in this way is called an **emulsion**.

Water experiment

MAKE AN EMULSION!

1 Fill the bottle a quarter full with water.

2 Add the same amount of cooking oil.

3 Screw the cap tightly on the bottle. Shake the bottle hard up and down.

You need
- A medium-sized empty medicine bottle with a tightly fitting cap
- Cooking oil
- Water

The oil and water form a mixture called an emulsion. If you leave the emulsion standing, it will gradually separate into oil and water. Try adding a drop of detergent and then shaking the bottle again. The emulsion separates much more slowly now.

Three droppers, each with a different coloured ink, are squeezed into a tank of water.

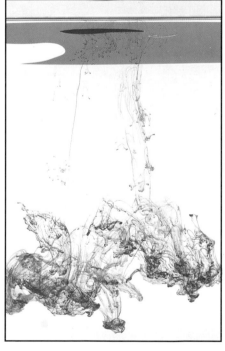

The drops of ink are heavier than water and sink. As they sink they stir up the water, which breaks them up.

The broken drops stir up more water, which makes them spread in all directions. This is how rain mixes with pond water.

15

Flowing

Water flows down mountainsides in rivers and waterfalls, and flows out of a jug when you pour it. It also flows out of taps into your bath. **Gravity** is the force on Earth that pulls everything downwards. Gravity makes water flow.

When you stand by a big waterfall you can get an idea of the enormous power of falling water. It pours down, thundering and pounding all day and night. As it flows down mountains it wears away the rocks, making valleys. It grinds rocks into smooth pebbles. And it carries away tonnes and tonnes of **silt** – finely ground rocks and sand.

Water work

Fast streams and rivers take many thousands of years to carve deep valleys. Trees and plants hold the soil together with their roots and stop it being washed away. When people cut down trees and let sheep and goats eat all the grass, soil that has taken hundreds of years to form can be washed away in one heavy storm.

Water squirts from this frog in a jet that is pulled downwards by gravity.

16

Did you know?

The highest waterfall in the world is the Angel Fall on the River Carrao in Venezuela. It has a drop of 979 metres.

Water experiment

WATER WHEELIES!

1 Cut a 7cm section from the drinking straw.

2 Cut slits round the edge of the plastic lid. Make a hole in the centre and push the straw through.

3 Bend the cut sections over, all at the same angle. Push the skewer through the straw. Hold the water wheel under a gently running tap and it will whizz round!

Water power

Streams and rivers rushing down mountains have lots of energy. If the water can be made to drive a wheel, the energy can be used to do work such as making electricity. The water can be trapped and stored in huge dams. Water is let out of the dams at a steady rate to drive electricity generators.

The energy in this flowing stream turns the wheel which drives machinery in the mill.

The Hoover Dam on the Colorado River, USA, can generate over 1,300 megawatts of electric power.

17

Spinning

When water is spun around, it moves away from the centre towards the outside. You can see this if you take a stick and stir water in a bucket. The water starts to climb up the sides of the bucket, leaving a dip in the centre. Water sometimes behaves like this naturally in fast rivers, making **whirlpools**. There are sometimes whirlpools in the sea, where strong currents flow between islands. Small boats can be tossed about and sunk if they get trapped in a big whirlpool.

Down the plughole

When water flows down between stones or out of a bath through the plughole, it sometimes makes such a powerful whirlpool that air is sucked down underwater. The air goes down inside a thin tube of spinning water.

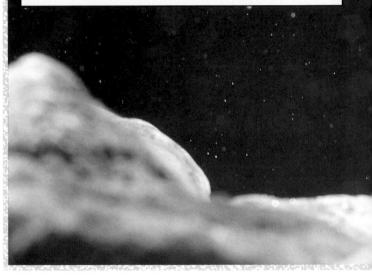

Most water spouts are about 8 metres across and around 100 metres high.

Water spout

A whirlwind is air that is spinning very fast. Whirlwinds over land suck up dust and sand. Over the sea they suck up water into water spouts. It is said that little fish are sometimes sucked up with the water and come down in salty rain – but this is probably just a tall story.

Sprinkler

When water squirts from a garden sprinkler, the force of the water jets sends the sprinkler whirling round. As the water spins round, the drops fly away from the centre.

A small whirlpool in a stream sucks air down in a tube of spinning water.

Did you know?

If you stir up sand in a jar of water, it will settle in a pyramid at the bottom.

Water experiment

GLUG OR NO GLUG?

1 Fill both bottles with water.

2 On the word "go", get your friend to empty one bottle while you empty yours.

3 If you hold your bottle upside down and swirl it around, a whirlpool will form inside it and it will empty much more quickly than your friend's.

You need
- *Two bottles*
- *A friend*

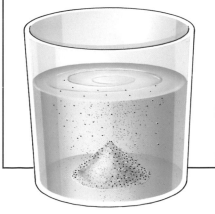

19

Surface

Some insects can walk on the surface of water. This is because water has a very thin stretchy skin on the surface. The skin forms because water is made up of tiny parts, called **molecules**, that are attracted to each other. Water molecules at the surface are more attracted to the water molecules below them than they are to the air, so they get pulled down slightly. This is  called **surface tension**. As a result, a stretchy skin is formed. It is surface tension that makes drops of water form into round shapes and holds a jet of water together.

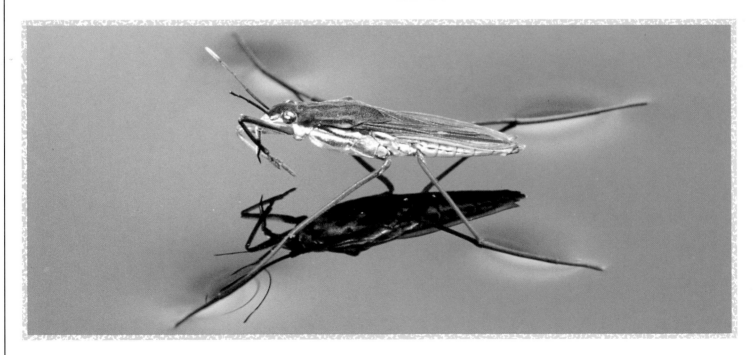

Surface dwellers

This pond skater is making dimples in the water where its feet press down on the pond's surface layer.

When streams become polluted with detergent, this layer is changed and surface dwelling insects can no longer live there.

Breaking the surface

Wind makes waves on the surface of the sea. Big waves travel for hundreds of kilometres across the ocean. When they reach shallow water near land, they are slowed at the bottom but keep going at the top, so they just fall over.

Water experiment

SKIMMING BEADS!

1 Fill the washing-up bowl with water and stir in a few drops of detergent without making too many bubbles.

2 Dip some water out of the bowl with the jug. Pour water gently over the back of a spoon, holding it about 1cm above the surface of the water.

Drips from the spoon form shining beads which glide over the surface. These are not bubbles.

You need
- A plastic washing-up bowl
- A jug
- Washing-up liquid
- A spoon

Water beads

You can sometimes see shiny beads of water skating over the surface of a stream near a waterfall.

These beads are formed by surface tension. Each one lasts for only a second or two.

21

Soaking up

If you dip one corner of a sponge into water and leave it there, the whole sponge will gradually become sodden. This is because sponges are full of tiny holes which draw the water up. But what makes water soak into the holes in this way?

To understand this, you have to know what a **capillary** is. A capillary is a very thin tube. When the end of a capillary is put into water, the water is pulled up inside the tube. The tiny holes in a sponge are capillaries, so water gets drawn into them until the sponge is full. Water soaks into blotting paper because the gaps between the paper **fibers** act as capillaries.

Capillary tubes

Thin glass tubes arranged in order of size have been dipped into colored water. The pull of surface tension makes water rise in the tubes. It rises highest in the thinnest tube because this contains the least weight of water. If you look closely at the surface of the water in the tubes, you will see it is not flat but curved, like a saucer.

Put a stick of celery into a jar of water containing a few drops of red food coloring. Leave it for a few hours.

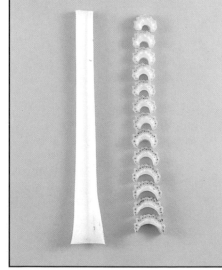

If you cut the stalk into several sections, you can see how far the dyed water has been soaked up.

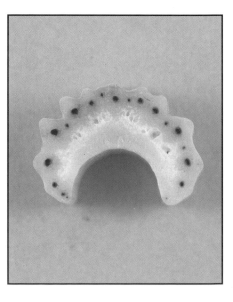

As the dye is soaked up, it colors the dots in the sections red. Each red dot contains about 50 capillaries.

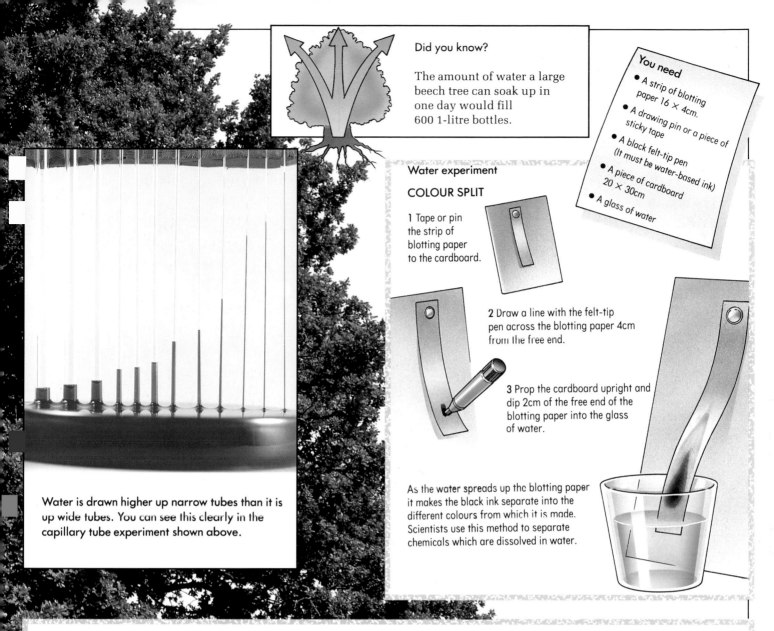

Did you know?

The amount of water a large beech tree can soak up in one day would fill 600 1-litre bottles.

You need
- A strip of blotting paper 16 × 4cm.
- A drawing pin or a piece of sticky tape
- A black felt-tip pen (It must be water-based ink)
- A piece of cardboard 20 × 30cm
- A glass of water

Water experiment

COLOUR SPLIT

1 Tape or pin the strip of blotting paper to the cardboard.

2 Draw a line with the felt-tip pen across the blotting paper 4cm from the free end.

3 Prop the cardboard upright and dip 2cm of the free end of the blotting paper into the glass of water.

As the water spreads up the blotting paper it makes the black ink separate into the different colours from which it is made. Scientists use this method to separate chemicals which are dissolved in water.

Water is drawn higher up narrow tubes than it is up wide tubes. You can see this clearly in the capillary tube experiment shown above.

The wood of a tree, like this oak, contains many capillaries. You can see them as tiny holes.

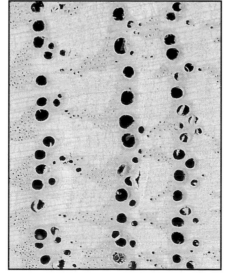

If you look at the holes through a powerful microscope, you will see that they are round tubes.

Thirsty plants

Plants take in water from the soil through their roots. As water evaporates through tiny holes underneath the plant's leaves, more water gets drawn up through the plant's stem or trunk. It is a long way for water to travel from the roots of a tree to the leaves at the top. The roots help by "pushing" water up the trunk.

Floating

Fill a jug with water right to the brim. Hold a cup under the jug's lip to catch any water that spills out and gently float something in the jug, perhaps a small jar. It doesn't matter what you float, it will always push out its own weight in water. This fact was discovered more than 2,000 years ago by Archimedes, a Greek scientist. He discovered it when he sat down in a full bath. He ran into the street shouting "Eureka!" (I have found it).

The Dead Sea is so salty that people can float in it with their arms out of the water.

Air trapped in the ducklings' feathers makes them float more than half out of the water.

How dense can you get?

Imagine a cube of water – like a sugar cube – with each side 1 centimetre long. This is called a **cubic centimetre** (1 cc) of water and weighs exactly 1 gram (1g). If you dissolve salt in 1 cc of water, it weighs more than 1g because the water is denser.

Things float more easily in a dense liquid. The water of the Dead Sea contains so much salt that people can float in it easily. Mercury is a liquid metal that is thirteen times more dense than water. Stones float in it like corks in water.

Water experiment

EGG-STRAORDINARY!

1 Fill the glass with water and put in the egg, which will sink.

You need
- An egg
- Salt
- A teaspoon
- A glass of water

2 Add 3 or 4 teaspoons of salt and stir gently. The egg should then float. If it does not, add more salt.

The egg floats because salt water is more dense than fresh water.

What happens if you gently pour more fresh water over the floating egg?

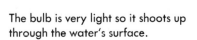

A light bulb released under the water floats up quickly.

The bulb is very light so it shoots up through the water's surface.

It takes a lot of water with it and makes a big splash.

Drips and drops

Imagine a rain drop falling from a cloud. It starts off tiny and just drifts downwards. As it falls it gets bigger and comes down faster. Surface tension (see pages 20 and 21) is trying to pull it into a perfectly round shape. But as it rushes down through the air, air resistance is trying to flatten it. When the drop grows to about 5mm across, surface tension can't hold it together any more and it breaks into smaller drops. Each of these may then start to grow again. Drips from a tap do not get big enough or fall fast enough for air resistance to break them up.

Spikes

When a small raindrop falls onto a pond it makes a hole in the surface that quickly fills with water. The water tries so hard to fill the hole that it rises up into a spike. Then the spike breaks up into two or three little drops.

Did you know?

The flatter the surface on which a water drop forms, the larger the drop – up to about 4mm.

You need

● An eye dropper

● A bowl of water

Water experiment

SPIKES OR BUBBLES?

1 Fill the eye dropper with water.

2 Hold the dropper high above the bowl of water and squeeze out one drop at a time. What shape do the drops make when they hit the water?

3 Now hold the dropper lower and try the experiment again. Can you see any difference in the shape made by the drops when they hit the water from different heights?

Surface bubbles

When a large raindrop falls on a pond it makes a big hole in the water. This time there is no spike of water. Instead, a bubble, lasting just a few seconds, appears on the surface. That is because the water has closed over the hole, trapping air beneath the surface. Look out for spikes and bubbles next time you are near a pond or puddle in the rain.

Bubbles

Bubbles are pockets of gas. They are round for the same reason that raindrops are round, for both are shaped by surface tension (see pages 20 and 21). A bubble rising through water is rather like a falling raindrop. Surface tension inside the bubble tries to keep it a round shape, but water resistance outside pushes it into a flat shape. If a rising bubble is too big, water resistance breaks it up into smaller bubbles. Soap bubbles floating in air are made of a thin skin of water.

Gas bubbles rushing to a pond's surface from dead leaves.

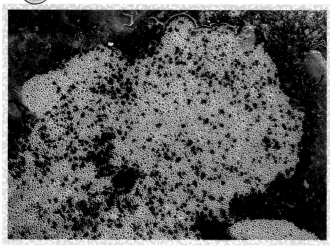

Tadpoles make froth, which is lots of tiny bubbles. The froth lasts because of slime in the water.

Natural gas

Dead leaves at the bottom of a pond sometimes rot and produce marsh gas. This has hydrogen in it and when lit burns with a blue flame. When it burns, oxygen in the air joins with the hydrogen, and guess what it makes – water! (see p.5)

Detergent bubbles squeezed together are no longer round. They may have five or seven sides, but most have six, like honeycomb.

Fizzy pop

Pressure makes gas dissolve. Fizzy drinks are full of dissolved **carbon dioxide** gas. It has been put in under pressure. Opening the bottle releases the pressure, so the gas bubbles out of solution. If you open the top slowly, you can hear it hissing out.

Water experiment

THE AMAZING BOUNCING LENTILS!

1 Fill the jug three-quarters full of water. Add an eggcup of vinegar and two teaspoons of bicarbonate of soda. Gently stir the mixture to get rid of the froth.

2 Drop in a teaspoon of lentils, which will sink. Soon they will start to move – first rising to the surface then sinking again. They will continue to do this for some time.

Gas bubbles form on the lentils. The bubbles make the lentils rise to the surface. At the surface the bubbles burst and the lentils sink to the bottom again.

You need
- A glass jug
- An egg cup
- A teaspoon
- Vinegar
- Bicarbonate of soda
- Lentils

Warning!
Ask an adult to help you with this experiment.

Depth

The deeper you go underwater, the greater the water pressure. About 6.2 miles (10km) under the ocean the pressure is more than about 1.1 tons for .155 square inch (1 metric ton for every square cm). Some animals can live there without being squashed because their bodies are made of liquids and solids that cannot be **compressed**. This means they cannot be squeezed smaller. But if you bring these creatures to the surface they swell up as dissolved gases in their bodies form bubbles.

Fish have swim bladders to help them rise or sink in the water.

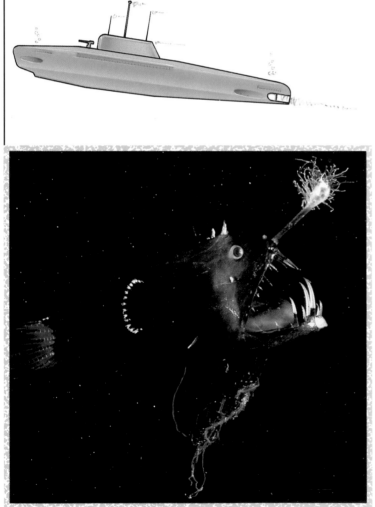

This angler fish lives in the depths of the ocean. Its body can withstand the great pressure of the water.

Rising and falling

Divers and submarines rise in the sea by making themselves lighter. To sink, they make themselves heavier. Fish rise and fall using a special air-filled bag inside their bodies called a **swim bladder**. This is filled with air and makes the fish float. To sink, the fish draws some of the air out of the bladder into its blood. Air-breathing sea creatures, such as turtles, do not have swim bladders. They have to work hard to swim down from the surface.

Water experiment

THE DIVING PEN TOP

You need
- A pen top
- Plasticine
- Plastic bottle
- A glass
- Water

1 Make the diver from a pen top by weighting the bottom rim with a piece of Plasticine. DO NOT BLOCK THE HOLE.

If there is a small air hole at the *other* end of the pen top, block it up with Plasticine.

2 Adjust the amount of Plasticine until the diver just floats in a glass of water.

3 Drop the pen top gently into a plastic bottle ¾ filled with water. Screw the lid on tightly.

4 Squeeze the bottle gently and the diver sinks. Release the bottle and it rises again.

The weight of water

The human body cannot survive deep under water without special equipment to protect it from the great pressure. Divers wear thick suits and have air pumped down to them at the same pressure as the water where they are working. For really deep dives, people have to go in submarines made of strong metal with very thick glass windows that can withstand tremendous pressure.

Submarines are built to withstand the tremendous pressure of the deep sea.

Deep-sea divers have special suits to protect them from the pressure of the water.

Water words

Capillary A very thin tube.

Carbon dioxide A gas made of oxygen and carbon. We breathe out carbon dioxide.

Compress To squeeze something and make it smaller.

Condense To change from a vapour to a liquid.

Cubic centimetre A cube with each side 1cm long.

Dissolve To mix completely with a liquid.

Drizzle Very fine rain.

Emulsion A mixture of tiny globules of oil and water.

Evaporate To change from a liquid to vapour.

Fibres Tiny threads.

Geyser A spout of steam and hot water from under the ground.

Glacier A river of ice.

Globule A small round drop of liquid.

Gravity The force that pulls objects back towards Earth.

Hydrogen A gas found in water and in all plants and animals.

Molecule The smallest amount of a chemical substance that can exist by itself. Every water molecule contains two atoms of hydrogen and one atom of oxygen.

Oxygen A gas found in water, the air and all living things. We take in oxygen when we breathe.

Sediment Solid particles that sink to the bottom of a liquid.

Silt Finely ground-up rocks and mud carried along by rivers.

Solution A solid or gas mixed completely with a liquid.

Surface tension A force that pulls the surface of liquids down, making a thin skin on top.

Swim bladder An air-filled bag inside a fish's body that enables it to rise and fall in the water.

Water vapour A mass of tiny drops of water in the air.

Waterproof Having a surface that water cannot pass through.

Whirlpool Water spinning round.

Index

Picture credits

All photographs are by Kim Taylor and Jane Burton except for Zefa title page, 4-5, 17 bottom right, 20-21; Tony Stone 4 bottom left, 24; World Wide 4 inset left; Bruce Coleman 4 inset right, 7, 8 bottom left and right, 10 bottom left, 12, 16-17, 17 bottom left, 22-23 background; Science Photo Library 13, 18; Planet Earth Pictures 30 bottom left and right; Aspect Pictures 31.